LIFE PLANNING

LIFE PLANNING

Paul H. Dunn & Richard M. Eyre

Bookcraft
Salt Lake City, Utah

Library of Congress Catalog Card Number:
79-52230
ISBN 0-88494-374-7

4th Printing, 1982

Lithographed in the United States of America
PUBLISHERS PRESS
Salt Lake City, Utah

Contents

Introduction *1*

Some Examples 23

Life Planning 45

Review of Principles 95

INTRODUCTION

Introducing, in order of appearance, the main characters in the drama of Life Planning: Earth, Time, Planning, *and* Faith,

We can understand the drama of Life Planning better (and enjoy it more) if we are somewhat acquainted with the players who have the lead roles. We have all met Earth, Time, Planning, *and* Faith, *but perhaps we can come to know them better by viewing each of them in two or three new ways. . . .*

Earth *(View 1)*

Have you ever thought of our earth as a great   5
laboratory? It is the most perfectly designed
laboratory ever built. Every necessary element is
available, everything needed is at hand for
conducting a great experiment: laws, choices,
agency. What is the purpose of the
experiment? Simply this: that we might discover
true joy and have it in great abundance.

We each have the opportunity to conduct our
own experiment.

The raw material we work with is *time*, and we are
to turn it into joy and purpose. The tools are
our physical selves, our senses. The ingredients are
air and mountains, grass and flowers, the
earth and all it contains.

There are resistors, of course—impurities, false
information—things that can cause our
experiment to fail.

And there are also laws—not to restrict our
experiment, but to tell us precisely how to
run it, how to make it succeed.

The Supervisor of our orbiting laboratory is too
wise to conduct our experiment for us. He
knows that freedom is the requisite of all true
learning. And the two destroyers of freedom

are *compulsion* (no chance to choose) and *ignorance* (no knowledge of options).

The Supervisor safeguards our freedom by sweeping both aside. He removes (or allows us to remove) ignorance by putting all necessary truth in the lab. He removes compulsion by not making that truth too obvious or too easy, by allowing opposing (even destructive) forces to operate in the lab. Thus he wisely refuses to prevent injury at the expense of learning.

6

One factor that makes this laboratory different from any other is that its elements, in addition to being acted upon *by us*, can also act *on us*. They are not passive but active, not stable but volatile. Envy, greed, love, hate, passion, peace—they don't wait in their test tubes for us to mix and match them; they create their own force fields and will experiment with *us* if we fail to learn how to control *them*.

In the end, if we succeed and turn time into joy, the Supervisor (who has *lent* us all we need for the experiment) remakes the laboratory, removes its defects and dangers, and *gives* it to us—together with the time, together with the joy.

Time (View 1)

How would you like to try to learn to be a catcher
without a ball? How would you like to plant without
seeds or to sing without a voice?

How would you like to plan without time?

We *cannot* plan without time.

Planning is the secret and the key to success.
It is the only way to achieve, to grow, to reach. It is
the only way we can proceed upon the Father's
decreed course of eternal progression.

Time is the element in which we work out our
plans.

It is time, and the *passage* and *irretrievability*
of time, that makes deadlines and objectives and
goals meaningful.

Without time we have nothing.

Without time planning is nonsense.

But we do have time. Our finite earth, in its
finite solar system, exists in *time*.

Finity separates the infinities.

Time separates our first eternity from our second
eternity, both of which are timeless. And yet

they *contain* time, endless time, which can offer us endless progress.

If we learn to use time.

Earth is where we learn that.

Planning *(View 1)*

There *is* more time available to those who are always   9
wishing for more. It's hiding, camouflaged so well
that we can't see it even though it's right under
our noses.

There are 168 hours each week (in *every* week). If
you add up all the time you can account for in a
week (sleeping time, eating, working, traveling,
reading, leisure, television, praying, family,
meetings) you won't even get close to 168. There will
be 20 or 30 hours that you can't find, and there
will be another 10 or 15 (or more) that you'll realize
you wasted. There are as many hours in your
day (exactly) as in the U.S. President's, as in the
prophet's.

The key is to "uncamouflage" our time, to
paint it so it can't hide or slip away unnoticed. We do
that through *planning*.

Earth *(View 2)*

10   We can:
Do more than look—we can *observe*.
Do more than read—we can *absorb*.
Do more than hear—we can *listen*.
Do more than listen—we can *understand*.
Do more than touch—we can *feel*.
Do more than exist—we can *live*.
Do more than live—we can *love*.
Do more than talk—we can *say something*.
Do more than work—we can *serve*.

Life on this earth can be lived on so many different levels. The conversion factor of time into joy can be almost 100 percent. Every moment contains joy—if we know the laws that extract it.

Next time you pass a rosebush in bloom without stopping to smell, ask yourself (honestly) if the place you're rushing to get to will give you more joy than what you've just passed up.

Time (View 2)

Richard Eyre remembers sitting for breakfast in a   11
grand old hotel in Salzburg, in historic Austria:

On business, I am trying to squeeze an extra
morning into the trip to finish some writing
and reading, grateful for the half day between
responsibilities, eating quickly, needing the
time.

Next to me sits an old woman, wealthy but lonely,
needing to talk. Five minutes reveals her
situation—widowed, alone, wintering in a warm
place. . . . "I'm letting the hems down in all
my dresses," she says. "It passes the time."

I'm upstairs now, in my room, using part of my half
day to write this. I'm thinking, she and I are
so totally different, yet we have one thing totally in
common: Time is our enemy. It's hers because
she has too much each day; it's mine because I have
too little.

It would all be solved if she could just give me
some of her time each day. (What I couldn't do with
two extra hours each day! I'd finish my
manuscripts, have that time with my family. . . . Can
you imagine—two full hours, free, every day.
And she would never miss it! In fact, it would help
her—she'd have less time to try to pass.)

But you know, she wouldn't sell even an hour. No one would.

It all reminds me of the last words of Queen Elizabeth I: "I would give all my possessions for a moment of time."

Planning (View 2)

A speaker once posed the question of whether it is best to live a "planned life" or a "spontaneous life."

13

That seems to be like asking whether it is best to create an oil painting with a brush or with paint. Planning and spontaneity are not enemies or opposites or competitors. They are teammates and partners.

The requirements for spontaneity are the *freedom* of an ordered, uncluttered mind (so that opportunities are noticed), and *confidence* (so that opportunities are seized). Clear goals and good planning produce both.

Faith (View 1)

14   "Now faith is the *substance*...," begins Hebrews 11.

Faith is power. Can power be substance?

Joseph Smith said, "When a man works by faith he works by mental exertion instead of physical force." And he said elsewhere, "Working by faith is easy, but it requires constant mental effort." Still elsewhere he said, "When we learn how to come to Him (God), He begins to open the heavens to us and to tell us all about it."

There is something so powerful in faith that no mortal can fully understand it. (Some *use* it, but none fully comprehend.) Faith is the power by which the worlds were made. It connects us, somehow, to the veil, to the *reason* for this memoryless earth.

We are here to *learn*. We must learn choices and parenthood and control of matter. But perhaps most important of all, we're here to learn *faith*! We're here to develop this greatest of all powers, this singular, real *substance* without which we cannot achieve our full potential.

Faith is similar to but the opposite of confidence. It says "yes"—but not because "I can do it." It says "yes" because "I *can't* do it alone" (inadequacy yields humility yields faith). Faith combines belief (that it can *and* that it will happen) with sincerity, with real intent.

Faith is the way in which we must come to God.

A prayer with faith is totally unrelated to a prayer without faith. They are different altogether. One is power and reality; the other is surface and shadow.

Faith *(View 2)*

16   Richard Eyre relates:

The phone rang one day, and when I picked it
up I heard almost hysterical sobbing. "I'm in such
pain. *Pray* for me, please. Pray now."

This sister in the ward had cut her leg badly in
the previous week. It must be infected.

"Sister, don't worry, I'll say a prayer. And I'll find
your daughter and bring her by to care for you."
I bowed my head, said a brief prayer, sincere and
with intent. I found the daughter, took her
home, went back to what I was doing.

Half an hour later the phone rang again. It was the
same voice, only worse, more hysterical.
"Please *pray* for me. Please pray for me."

I became more worried then, so I got more
practical: "Sister, what is your doctor's
number?"

"He's out. They can't find him. *Pray* for me."

"I will. Give me his number. I'll get him over there."
I tracked the doctor down, got *him* worried. He
said he'd be there in an hour. I hung up, but the
words rang in my mind: "Pray for me." My
wife had just come in—we knelt there on the

kitchen floor with two of our children. *Mental exertion*—this time I *exercised, summoned* faith: "Father, you can alleviate pain; there is real need here; I believe you will."

Sincerity and real intent were present, as in the earlier prayer—but this time faith was also there, there by mental exertion.

I knew as I prayed that I was heard, because that soft, still, sure, simple feeling said, "Yes."

An hour later the phone rang again. The sister again—she was calm now. I asked, "Did the doctor come?"

"Yes, but I didn't need him. The pain went away. You must have prayed."

It was a small incident. But now I *know* (more than before)—
the difference between the first and second prayer;
the difference between no faith and faith;
the difference between surface and depth;
the difference between no power and power.

E*arth (View 3)*

18   Alma effectively described faith by using the
analogy of a seed. (See Alma 32.) Many prophets
have explained the beautiful connections between
ancestors and descendants through the object
lesson of the roots and branches of a tree. The
Master himself opens the vision of God's
eternal fatherhood and his own saviorship by using
comparisons involving shepherds and sheep.
He helps us understand the kingdom of God by
comparing it to a treasure hidden in a field,
to a pearl of great price, to a net cast into the sea.

Think about it: Could we understand faith as well
if there were no seeds? families, if there were
no trees? ourselves as children, if there were no
sheep? the kingdom, if there were no treasures
or pearls or nets in the seas?

This incredible earth, as well as being the *place* of
great learning, is the *source* and *subject matter* of
great learning. The world abounds with object
lessons. Every aspect of nature teaches us
truths that go far beyond nature itself. And the
world itself is the largest of all object lessons. It
was born; it was baptized by water and renewed; it
will be baptized by fire and glorified.

Perhaps spiritual truths contain such
connections and complexities that we children
cannot effectively grasp or learn them

without the help of a simpler, temporal analogy
here, on this mother earth.

We need not wonder at these things. The
earth is our school and our school*master*. It is our
home now; if we learn, it will be our home for
eternity.

Time (View 3)

20   The words of a widely seen film: *"Life offers you two precious gifts: one is time; the other is the freedom to buy with that time what you will."* (From *Man's Search for Happiness*.)

Time is the unique gift of earthly life. Time separates eternity into timeless premortal existence and timeless after-life. Time is the device God gives us to expedite our growth and learning. Time teaches us the law of the harvest and the law of natural consequence.

Earth's time is so precious because it is so unique: It is the only time in eternity with *time*, with limits. The challenge of our lives is to learn to use time.

Planning and Faith (View 3)

True planning *is* faith. "When we work by faith we 21
work by mental exertion." Faith is not merely
asking, or hoping, or believing. It is *exercising* the
mind on how a thing can be obtained. (The
brother of Jared showed faith, not when he asked
the Lord how to light the ships but when he
presented the clear stones. Oliver Cowdery couldn't
translate when he "took no thought [but] to
ask"—D&C 9:7.)

Whatever the mind of man can *conceive* and *believe*,
it can *achieve*. When a goal is firmly set, a plan
clearly laid—prayerfully, faithfully, as well as
thoughtfully—it is then both *conceived* and
believed. Work has been done by mental exertion;
faith has been exercised and summoned;
and thus the goal will be *achieved*.

We often taught our missionaries that a mission is
life in miniature. When time is not well
planned and well used, a mission slips away like
quicksilver, with little result left behind and
little growth carried ahead. But when missionaries
make effective use of prayerfully set goals
and plans, an almost unbelievable amount is
accomplished in two short years, and a
foundation for life is laid.

A mission is a microcosm of life, for indeed, a *life* is
short, a *life* ends at a particular point, a *life*

contains a limited amount of incredibly precious time over which we are stewards.

The lives of men without goals and plans slip by like shadows, leaving no trace, no legacy, and taking away no learning, no growth. Other lives, blueprint-built rather than random-spent, leave traces in time and carry away light and power for the journey into the next world.

SOME
EXAMPLES

*Real-life stories
about you and me,
and about why we need
to plan our lives.*

From Real Life

When we talk about earth and time and planning   25
and faith, we're talking about things that affect
us; we're talking about elements of mortality that
can and should make a difference in our
lives. This section will demonstrate what we mean.
In the following pages we'll take a look at
people who are in just about every situation of
life—people who are in circumstances like
yours and ours.

As you read about these people, look for yourself
in them. You may see yourself more than
once. And you'll certainly see that their needs are
in many ways your needs, because all of us, no
matter what our situation, need life planning.

Here, then, are some real-life examples of why we
need to plan our time and our lives. If you read
one of these examples and say, "Hey, that's me!" be
grateful that we didn't *say* it was you! We've
changed the names to protect the guilty!

The College Freshman

26   Cindy started her freshman year last October. It's Christmastime now, and she's back home thinking about those first three months and wondering why it wasn't all that she had dreamed it would be. Oh, she had a good time, and she certainly feels that her eyes were opened a bit, but something bothers her, and she is trying to sort out just what it is. Her parents aren't much help; she found out on the first night back that their main interest is whether she's been getting in by dorm hours and how her grades look so far.

Cindy knows that those things were not the problem. It had more to do with her surroundings and *observations* at school. She had one roommate who was waiting for a missionary and thought about nothing else. Another one had never had anything but A's and cared only about maintaining her record. The third was a shy girl from a small town who just did what she was told and seemed never to have a thought of her own. The fourth was what Cindy categorized as a "scatterbrained socialite" who thought mostly about parties and boys and "popularity." The only roommate who really seemed to think for herself was a girl named Sue, who was disillusioned with quite a few things and was trying hard, in her own way, to sort out her life through Eastern philosophy and a few soft drugs.

At least part of the question in Cindy's mind, as she thinks about it during the holidays, is where she is going. She knows that her father, proud of her good grades and high I.Q., wants her to be a doctor. She knows that her mother basically wants her just to mark time and do well until "Mr. Right" comes along and marries her. Part of the problem, she decides, is the wide difference in the way the two of them see her. But the real problem, the root, is not what *they* want Cindy to be. The real problem is the fact that Cindy doesn't know what *she* wants to be. She smiles as she thinks about it; it's the "identify identification problem" that her psychology professor was talking about the other day—the professor who seems to Cindy to be more confused than the kids he teaches.

She thinks on: it's interesting that when you're living at home, going to high school, you know who you are, and you know where you're going. You're so-and-so's daughter, and you're a cheerleader, and you're the vice-president of your seminary class. And where are you going? Well, you're going to college of course. Everything is very secure, very simple.

Now, all of a sudden, the *questions* change. It's not just who you are, but who you are going to be; it's not just where you're going, it's how and when you're going to get there.

Cindy is perplexed. She feels like someone who has been cast adrift, put in a boat and shoved out to sea not knowing where the destination is, not even knowing how to sail.

The Frazzled Father

28   Terry and his wife, Marcie, had their second child
last week. Terry finished graduate school two years
ago and by almost any measurement is doing
extremely well. He's had two promotions in the last
month; he finalized the mortgage on a new
home just three weeks ago; and the vice-president
of his company pulled him aside just yesterday
and, after congratulating him on the new baby, said,
"We've got our eye on you, young man. Just
keep up the good work!"

Terry leaves tomorrow for a two-week "intensive
learning" seminar sponsored by his
industry, held in New York. In a way he hates to
leave Marcie and the new baby so soon, but the
seminar is held only once a year and Marcie's
mother will come over. And it appears as if,
with a little luck and with a good word or two from
the right people, he can parlay that seminar
experience into a shot at the assistant division
manager's job that is coming open next
winter.

Terry is on a fast track and he knows it. It's amazing
how one thing seems to lead to another and
how a little favor for someone in the company can
get you a good word just when you need it. And
besides, it's great for Marcie too. Even though he's
seeing a little less of her lately, he's planning
to surprise her on Christmas by telling her that the

Ford is hers—all hers, because he's buying a
little sports car to commute in. (It's better on gas
anyway, and it just might catch the eye of one
or two people that "need" to have a little more
definite *impression* of Terry.)

Terry's not available for church *every*
Sunday, but then who is, really? There was that one
calling he couldn't accept, but they called John
and he's probably better for it anyway. Terry figures
that a real reputation and some recognized
accomplishments and positions in his field will
greatly enhance his ability to influence people
for good and make real, *significant* contributions in
the Church a little later on when he has more
time.

The Returned Missionary

30   Vern returned from his mission three months ago.
He had served well, accomplished much and built a
strong personal testimony. It was hard leaving
the friends, the companions, and the *atmosphere* of
the mission field. At the same time, the
homecoming was exciting: the changes in people,
the changes they saw in him, the talks in
church, the general "fresh new look" at life.

That initial excitement is over now though, and
Vern feels the crush and depression of
insignificance. No one really seems to need him
here, at least not like in the field, and the
things he is doing are so mundane, so
unimportant. He isn't changing anyone's life,
he isn't giving any priceless gifts, he has no heavy,
bracing responsibilities. Oh, he tries to
continue his scripture study and to keep in touch
with old companions. And he is definitely trying
to keep doing missionary work. But it all seems so
"un-urgent." And the people around Vern,
especially his relatives, seem to treat him like the
Vern of two or three years ago rather than the
elder who had been relied on by so many such a
short time ago.

The other part of Vern's concern is the sudden
complexity of his life. In the mission field the
objective was so simple and so
straightforward: find those who will accept the

gospel; teach and baptize them. Now that
single dimension is replaced with a whole host of
concerns: finances, social life, school work,
job, church job, things at home, things with friends.
And those *decisions*—it's the decisions that really
get to Vern at times. Before, there was always the
mission coming up; all the really important
decisions seemed pretty far off, because they were
behind and beyond that mission.

But now he is home. He keeps wanting not to
acknowledge that fact. Too many decisions, *big*
ones, are staring him in the face. What to major
in, where to live, where to work, what career to
point towards, who to marry, how to
prioritize one important thing over another, how
to think effectively about all these things at
once. Vern dreams at night of being back on his
mission, and when he isn't asleep he often
finds himself lying awake yearning for the simplicity
and the fulfillment of the field.

Now, things aren't really *that* gloomy. Vern
has good times, and the freedom and choices feel
pretty good sometimes. He's aware, though,
that his prayers and spirituality are slipping a little,
that his confidence that he'll always be better
than average isn't quite so strong as it was. But then,
the mission field isn't a very realistic place
anyway, Vern says to himself, and perhaps it's just
best to take life as it comes. (Besides, the time
in between the *major* events of mission and marriage
isn't very important anyway, is it?)

The Aging "Young Man"

32   Jim is middle-aged. (Or should we say *other* people
would categorize him as middle-aged. Jim would
fight the idea to the death.) He jogs every
morning. He dresses like his eighteen-year-old son
(whom, Jim will remind you, he can still beat
in tennis). He tints his hair just enough to disguise
the grey; and if you discuss his career with him
he will tell you that he's just getting started. He'll
says he's considering several other options
presently and that his ultimate goal of running a
company really hasn't changed since he left
school (which, as he will probably *not* tell you, was
seventeen years ago).

Jim is scared. He is scared of time; because time
is robbing him—robbing him of his image, of his
youth, of his dreams. Jim had certain ideas
about where and what he would be by the time he
was forty—and since he isn't there yet, he
naturally can't allow himself to actually believe that
he is past forty yet. Jim's family is slipping
away. One daughter is already married (let's not
even *mention* the possibility of being a
grandfather; Jim would jog a long way to get away
from that thought). His son plans to go on a
mission next summer. Two other "children" are
already teenagers. It's only little six-year-old
Susan who puts Jim into the "young father"
category, where he feels most "natural."

The problem is—well, it's a paradox really—on
one hand Jim wants to be in the whirlpool and the
sauna with the older, senior executives of his
company, yet on the other hand he wants to be on
the ski slopes and tennis courts with the young
trainees just hired last fall.

His wife isn't as young as she used to be; it's easy for
Jim to see that. Again it's ironic: on one hand
he's pleased when people say he looks younger than
she. On the other hand he worries a lot about
her looks.

Jim can't dream quite like he used to. His life has
become too set; there are too many things he
has to do before he can even think about what he'd
like to do. Jim worries about this. He feels that
there is something great inside him, some gift, some
power, some noble uniqueness that's never
been recognized by anyone yet. He feels that inside
him is something that should make him more
than ordinary, that should make him more
"timeless" than "middle-aged." But what is
it? And how can he get at it?

The Retired Couple

34 Cyril and Belva are nearly a year into their
retirement. Cyril was forty years with a good firm,
and their retirement benefits make them
financially comfortable. In the past year they have
been to see each of their three children (and
families) at least once; they have also spent two
weeks in Hawaii.

Just last week a realtor called and made them
a pretty good offer on their house. It wasn't for sale
but apparently it had caught the eye of someone
with money, and Cyril and Belva are now thinking
somewhat seriously about selling the house
and getting a condominium in a warmer climate.
The only thing holding them back is the
Cullimores, their next-door neighbors and lifelong
friends. Bill Cullimore still has three years
left before his retirement, and they had always
talked about "doing it together."

Cyril and Belva both say they have never
been freer. It's so amazing, they both say, to be able
to just get up and go wherever the urge hits
them. They also say they have never felt better, that
never before have they felt that they had
enough time to read, or to sew, or to play golf, or to
do all the other things they've been waiting so
long to "get at."

One notices, though, that as they describe all the
things they've never had more of before, they

never mention the word *happiness* or *fulfillment* or
anything similar. It even seems that those
poor Cullimores who have to wait another three
years for their freedom are often happier than
they are. It's as though Cyril and Belva are sure
they have all the pieces to the happiness
puzzle now—certainly more than before—yet it
doesn't fit together quite as well as it did when
they *didn't* have all the pieces. One would have to say
that, after a year of the long-awaited
retirement, Cyril and Belva are a little perplexed.
They're not quite sure that this "autumn of our
years" is all that it was cracked up to be.

The Harried, Halted Housewife

36   Jane is thirty-three. She has been married now for
nearly fourteen years. She and her husband Phil
have four children, ranging in age from twelve to
three (and another one is on the way). They
live in a fairly nice house on a fairly nice street in a
fairly nice part of town. Phil has a good job; the
kids are healthy and reasonably happy; Jane teaches
Primary and is an officer in the PTA.

Everything is fine, really, except that Jane is
about to explode from frustration. Here's why (or
here are some of the reasons that Jane *thinks*
are why):

Jane didn't finish college and obtain her college
degree. Marriage prevented it, and she
spent three years (the last one with a baby) working
as a low-paid secretary to support Phil while he
finished school. That all seemed fine then; some of
her friends finished school, some didn't.
Jane was a talented artist and always imagined that
she would do something to develop her talent
later (a time and a season for everything she used to
say). She had also been a varsity debater and
had developed an active interest in politics. Phil had
often said during their courtship that she was
the one with the brains and the talent, and that if
they had any sense, she would finish school
and work and he would stay at home with the kids.
Those were the days before "women's

liberation" and before Jane had realized how
confining and stifling it was to be locked into
a life where she had to spend virtually all day, every
day, just trying to stay ahead of the domestic
chores.

But now things are different: now she knows! She
sees commercial artists with half her talent who
are doing better financially than her husband. She
sees that some of her own friends, who
limited their families to one or two children (or
none), are now starting careers of their own, or
championing causes of their own, or developing
talents of their own—anything, for heaven's
sake, *of their own*.

Jane stands by the sink now, doing the dishes (an
unending flow), gazing out of the window,
and wondering if the world will forever keep
passing her by.

The Ungratified Graduate

38   Elizabeth plants her left ski pole and kick-turns
intentionally out of the main run and into the
untracked powder. She skirts a small clump of
fir trees and side-skids to a stop in a stand of
white-barked aspens. She needs a moment to
think.

Karen, her best friend since childhood, and Karen's
new husband, Steve, have invited Liz to ski
with them for the day. She has accepted gladly
because for the three months since Karen's
wedding they have scarcely seen each other—quite
a trauma when you have literally lived with
someone for the past four years. This day,
however, has been a worse trauma still. Karen
is completely changed. Oh, she is still the same
person, and Liz loves her dearly, but her
interests and conversation are so different. The
whole conversation all the way up to the
mountain dealt with new home mortgages, and
grocery prices, and *children*. It all seems so
mundane to Liz. This is *Karen*. This is the person
who used to discuss the latest fashions, and
human rights issues, and the trip to Europe they
originally planned to take together this
winter. Everything changed on that night when they
both received their university degrees, Karen in
elementary ed and Liz in biology. It was later that
same night (while Liz was at the apartment
packing her bags) that Steve and Karen decided to
get married the next fall.

Liz is standing on her skis in the aspen grove
now, having a little conversation with herself, as she
often does. As usual, it's Liz (the free spirit, the
don't-tie-me-down feminist who wants a career)
versus Elizabeth (the practical,
let's-put-first-priorities-first Mormon who wishes
more than anything that the right guy would
come along).

Elizabeth: "You don't really think topics like grocery
prices and children are boring. You just wish
you had some reason to talk about them too. Face
it, what you're on edge about is that you
haven't found someone to share your life with yet.
You thought you would; all through college
you thought you would, but he never came along."

39

Liz: "No, it's you that's upset. You cling to that old
'marriage-will-solve-everything idea,' but deep
down you know that you want to experience some
things first, to use your education and your
talents. You're only twenty-two; there's plenty of
time. You just don't know what to do with it."

Elizabeth: "Well, at least we agree on one
thing: we're upset."

Liz: "Yes, and a little bit puzzled about why life
doesn't look as exciting right now as it ought
to."

On the way home that evening, Karen tells Liz that
she and Steve are expecting a baby in the fall.
Liz feels genuine happiness for them. She also feels
something else, something vaguely unpleasant
deep inside her, something she doesn't quite
understand.

The Man with Severed Moorings

40   Five weeks ago, James made this entry in his journal:

"What a day! Everything is going so well. I can't
really see any reason why I shouldn't get
Larry's position when he retires next month. I've
never been happier at work. June's pregnancy
is going fine. We've wanted this baby for such a long
time now; it's almost hard to believe that it
will be only another six months. The other kids are
doing really well. I'm just pleased with life right
now! I hope it lasts."

It didn't last. This is Jim's journal entry for today:

"What am I going to do? The roof has caved in. I feel
like a shipwrecked man without a life
preserver. I feel like I'm sinking. I've got nothing to
grab on to. I still can't believe they hired our
toughest competitor to fill Larry's slot. Once they
did that, it was a foregone conclusion that I'd
lose my job—after all, that guy and I have been
working against each other for eight years. I
probably could have handled that; after all, there
are other jobs—I'll find one—but when June
had the miscarriage the very next week. . . . Well,
since then I've just been spinning. I don't know
which way is up. I know it's the Lord that I need,
that we all need as a family. I'm praying like I
never have before, but I hardly know where to
start. I guess that's the word that scares me:

start. I'm not used to starting over; I'm not young enough to start over. Oh, what's the use! The more I write the worse things seem."

Jim pushes his journal aside and stares out the window into space. Well, he says to himself, at least I've got plenty of time—plenty of time to think.

The Transitional Teen

42   Craig turned eighteen today. It's Saturday, and he's going to celebrate with some friends later on. He opened some gifts from the family at supper and now finds himself alone in his room, looking at a note that came in the envelope from his grandparents—along with a check for $100. The note is lying on his desk, next to a thick, paperbound book. The note and the book are causing Craig to think pretty hard now—causing him to think about some things he has put off thinking about for quite a while.

The words on the cover of the book say, "Complete Listing of University Courses to be Offered in the Next Academic Year." The words on the note say: "For your mission. Love, Grandpop and Grandmom."

Craig has never told anyone that he is going to college. And he's never told anyone that he is going on a mission. The reason he hasn't told anyone is that he hasn't told himself. He will graduate from high school in three months and he is realizing now that the days beyond that graduation are as unknown and uncharted as the other side of the moon.

Life has been pretty easy for Craig, maybe too easy. He hasn't ever worried too much about anything because there hasn't ever been much to worry about. He has done reasonably well in school, and people tell him often that he'll go a long way on personality alone. When he thinks about it, he realizes that he's never fully applied himself to anything, except maybe the French horn. He's had four years of seminary and has always been active in the Church. And he *believes* it—or at least, as far as he knows he believes it.

Craig has the distinct feeling that things are changing, that things are getting more serious, that he really can't go much farther "on personality alone." Whether he likes it or not, he realizes time is marching on, and some things need to be thought about.

Well, enough of this gloom he thinks. It's my birthday! I'll start thinking tomorrow.

LIFE PLANNING

- *Understanding Life's General Purposes*
- *Understanding Your Life's Specific Purposes*
- *The Progressive Achievement of Goals*
- *Achievement Planning*
- *Relationship Planning*

Understanding Life's General Purposes

The previous section was about who we are. This section is about who we can become. What kind of people did we see in the examples just presented? We saw people who generally have good intentions, who deep down inside want to improve and grow but don't really know how to go about it. We saw people who share the essential elements of mortality—earth, time, planning ability, faith—but don't know how to use them.

But the Lord didn't intend for us to stumble blindly through this existence. He didn't intend for us to continually struggle against obstacles without ever making progress. He intended that we eventually become like him. And one way to help us do that is *life planning*. With *life planning* we can get a grip on ourselves!

To begin with, we must understand life's general purposes. We must realize what this existence is all about. A friend once asked a little four-year-old girl, "Where did we come from?" (Your only chance of getting a *simple* profound answer to a deep profound question is to ask a child.) She said, "From heaven." Then he asked, "Why did we come to this earth?" She said, "To have families." Not a bad answer for three words. Participating on this earth as children, then as parents, then as grandparents

in *families* is an extraordinary experience, an
experience of incredible learning. We are
here to *learn*. We learn to know God by taking the
role of *father*; we learn to know Christ by being
brothers to our fellowmen; we learn obedience by
becoming true *children* of God and of Christ.

We are here to find the other half of *joy*. (Half
of true joy, the half we already had, is to be, and
know that we are, children of God. The
other half is to demonstrate to ourselves that *we* can
learn and create and make choices and progress
and grow eternally until we become like him.) This
earth is designed to teach us that second
half—though we had to leave behind part of the
first half to come here. If we learn the second
half well, *full joy* will be ours when we are again back
with our Father. (See D&C 93:33-34 for the
Lord's words on this principle.)

We are here to experience things that were not
possible without physical bodies. These
bodies and this physical earth present us with
learning possibilities that did not exist before.
Like a wise father who lets his children go off to a
university because he knows they must face
obstacles and make their *own* decisions to truly
grow, so the wisest of fathers has sent us here.

Here we prove to ourselves what we are.
Here, in this brilliantly conceived "university" of
earth, we decide for ourselves what we
evermore will be.

Understanding Your Life's Specific Purposes

Into the "university" of earth comes a totally unique
individual, one with certain gifts, certain
abilities, and a particular *foreordination*, an outline
of purpose that is probably specific and
direct but is hidden behind the veil of mortality.

This individual is you! The problem is how to
discover that purpose, how to extract a clear
meaning from the confusion and blurred directions
of the world, how to find and link your
God-given gifts with the things you were sent here
to perform.

Giant airliners carry, as part of their
equipment, a tightly locked "black box" in which are
mechanisms that record every part of the
airplane's operation. If the plane crashes, the black
box usually contains the key to the misfunction.
Each of us has a "black box," a tightly locked (by the
veil) compartment somewhere in us that
contains all of who we are and all of who we can be.
Too often, like the airliner, its content is
unknown until after we crash, until our life is over,
and we discover, perhaps with
embarrassment and shame, where we went wrong,
what we should have done that we didn't, what
traits we could have developed but ignored.

Is it impossible to know the content of the "black
box" until our life is over? The answer is

no!—at least for those who have the gospel of Jesus Christ and are willing to search.

Here are some especially good places to start the search:

1. With Your Patriarchal Blessing

We have, in the restored Church, access to personal scripture, direct from God, relative to our callings and foreordination in life. The scripture is our patriarchal blessing. At its least, this blessing provides the recipient with indications as to the potentials he should perfect, the priorities he should pick, the principles he should practice, the paths he should pursue. At best, it gives him direct information about the callings and expectations that God has for his life.

A patriarchal blessing often seems to be a puzzle—and, in a way, it is meant to be so. Insight too easily gained is knowledge too seldom used. A blessing will yield its true meaning and specific interpretation only "line upon line, precept on precept" and only to one who *looks* and *thinks* and *asks*, with real intent, and with persistence and with faith.

2. Within Yourself, with Your "Gifts"

We are told that each of us has unique gifts; and it is implied that the identification of those gifts, along with their use and development, is essential to our exaltation.

You probably know more about what your gifts are than you realize. What are the things you are good at? What "comes easy" to you? What do you *enjoy* doing most? When you compare yourself with your friends, what areas do you feel most confident in?

What *spiritual* gifts do you have? (They're listed in D&C 46.) What *mental* gifts? What *social* gifts?

It's a wise idea to make a list. It's exciting to
realize what you are good at (though it may take a
few minutes of thinking to flush away the
self-doubts we often have, which make it initially
easier to recall what we are *not* good at).

A list of recognized "gifts" go with the
patriarchal blessing as the second keystone in one's
search for specific purpose.

*3. With Your Knowledge of Options (What Things
Are Available to You)*

All too often, we climb a mountain only to find, after
getting to the top, that it is not the right
mountain. (The engineer who suddenly realizes
he'd be happier as a doctor, the retired man
who now knows he should have worked another
five years, the career woman who wishes she'd
had children, the senior in biology who only now
discovers the more personally appealing
field of computer technology.) Life often presents
us with decisions before we are prepared to
make them, and we often make them before we
know or understand all the options.

A college student who is trying to decide on a
major ought to read the course catalog from cover to
cover, just to know his options. A man about
to retire ought to know (and weigh) all of the
possible things he could do after he retires, then
compare them to the things he could do if he kept
working. And so on and so on.

A list of options (free-thinking—without
self-imposed restrictions or limits) ought to go with
the patriarchal blessing and the "gifts list" as
tools in the task of knowing one's specific purposes.

4. With the Advice of Others

It is nearly impossible to truly see yourself without
a mirror. *Other people* are our mirrors. They can

tell us things about ourselves that we could be
incapable of seeing otherwise. It is critical, of
course, to find good and reliable mirrors. One with a
warp or a crooked plane will reflect untrue and
perhaps harmful images of ourselves. A good
"mirror," though, is invaluable; good advice
is as necessary to the growth of people as rain and
sun are to the growth of plants. The process of
making a "gifts list" and an "options list" is almost
impossible without the objective advice of
others.

Advice-seeking is an art. If done well, it can be not
only informative but fun, not only valuable
but enjoyable, not only helpful to you but helpful
to the person who gives the advice. Three
principles are involved:

a. *People are complimented and flattered when they are
asked for advice.* Someone asking for advice is
someone saying "I admire you so much that I want
to be like you." We should be, therefore, less
hesitant to ask for advice, even of someone we do
not know well.

The two types of people best equipped to
give us valuable advice are those who know us best
and those who know the most about the thing we
wish to become. The former are easily found
because they are the people closest to us. The
latter are easily found because they are the people
we admire most.

b. *Requests for advice should be specific.* If you
ask a busy man for fifteen minutes of his time
because "what you have done is so close to what I
hope to do; therefore, I need your advice," be sure
you have two or three specific questions that
you can quickly ask of him. Take notes on his
answers.

c. *Don't accept or use all the advice you receive.*
You will never get any *perfect* advice (at least not

from a mortal) so you'll have to weigh it against what *you* know and believe. Even "bad" advice is often helpful, because it stimulates our thought and gives us insight into the strength of what we already know. However, listening to people's advice and ideas can bring to light many opportunities.

You never know where, when or from whom you may learn something you can turn into great opportunity. Consider the following illustrations:

William Withering heard an old woman in Shropshire, England, tell how a flowering plant was good for dropsy. He followed up the idea and thus discovered digitalis, one of the most valuable drugs known in the treatment of heart disease.

Edward Jenner heard some dairymaids in his native Gloucester say that an unknown disease of cows protected against smallpox. He tested this seemingly impossible theory and discovered smallpox vaccination.

5. With Prayer

Only the Lord knows us completely. He wants (perhaps more than anything else) for us to find our purpose, and with it a fullness of joy. Yet he loves us too much to give it to us on a silver platter. That would thwart his ultimate purpose. Instead, he asks us to *ask*, and he tells us how to ask, and he tells us that the answers will not always be what we expect and will not always be given in the way we expect. (He also tells us that we ought to do a lot of thinking and searching before and during the time we ask.)

But the promise is clear, "Ask, and ye *shall* receive." (D&C 4:7; italics added.) Ask to know your purpose, to see your path, and the Lord (in his way and in his time) *will* show it to you.

Yes, we *can* know the content of our "black box," and the *first actual step* in *life planning* is to identify as much as possible what our specific purpose is, through these five sources and through *effort*, to put into *writing* all we can learn about the individual that each of us is and the foreordination each of us has.

Remember that God knows you not as one small percentage of mankind, but as an individual. We must strive to know ourselves in the same way.

The Progressive Achievement of Goals

The God and Father of us all has set for us a pattern   55
of "bringing things to pass." His use of goals and
plans (and his desire for *us* to master their use) is
apparent throughout the scriptures.

We know that the perfect order and beauty of
the earth resulted from the Lord's great master
plan, in which all things were created
spiritually before they were put physically upon the
earth. (See Moses 3:5.) We know that our
Heavenly Father meets *all* of his objectives—that
"there is nothing that the Lord . . . shall take
in his heart to do but what he will do it." (Abraham
3:17.) We also know that it is possible for *us* to
come to realize (as Paul did) that all of *our* righteous
goals can be met, that we can "do *all* things
through Christ which strengtheneth." (Philippians
4:13; italics added.)

The study of goals, in its ultimate sense, is
the study of God's power. The effort to perfect our
use of *life planning* is an effort to become more
like our Heavenly Father.

Walk into any big bookstore these days and you'll
find a whole wall full of "self-help" books. And
almost all of them have something to say about
goals. They agree that it's necessary to have
long-range goals before meaningful short-range
goals can be set. That's a true principle: you

need a target before you can have a bull's eye; you
need to know where the green is before you
can hit the tee shot.

One of the incalculable blessings of the gospel is a
knowledge of the longest-range goal. We
know that we can return, glorified, to the very
presence of God. Further, we know what is
necessary before we can do so. This simple but great
knowledge helps us in two vastly important
ways. First, the comforting thought that we can
actually "go back home" to a loving Father gives
us a "light at the end of the tunnel" in times when
all seems dark. Secondly, the knowledge of
our destination, if used properly, becomes a
backdrop for all our goals, a compass course
against which all our directions can be checked.

The word of the Lord, given through his prophets,
tells us in unmistakable terms that the
long-range goals of our life on earth must be to
come to know the Savior (and, through him,
the Father); to find and give true joy by serving
God and our fellowman and by being wise and
noble stewards over all that he entrusts us with; and
to build his kingdom—by building the
righteous subkingdoms of our own families and by
"feeding his sheep" with the gospel's truths.
These three goals were put simply into one
all-encompassing objective for life when
Christ said, "Come, follow me." (See Luke 18:22.)

Now, how do we go from there to the day-to-day?
How do we take that knowledge and that
desire and break it down into proportions that
influence us in specific ways at specific
moments? We do it one step at a time, and the *first
step* is described in the previous section:
study and *list* the directions your life should go, as
suggested by your patriarchal blessing, your
gifts, your options, the advice you have sought and
received, and by prayer. Let's call that "Step
1," and let's proceed now to move through the other

steps involved in *life planning*. As we do so, let's look again at one of the examples we looked at earlier; let's take Craig (you remember the young man trying to decide on college and on a mission), and use his life as an example to demonstrate these steps, one by one.

Craig's Story, Step 1

Craig resorts to life planning *to solve his dilemma and to find some purpose in his life. He knows he doesn't fully grasp his patriarchal blessing yet, but he makes a list of the things he can understand now. The list looks like this:*

Admonitions	Promises
• *through persistence and effort . . .*	• *. . . you will be successful in your studies and will obtain the knowledge necessary to have a successful career.*
• *through your diligence . . .*	• *. . . the way will be opened for you to become a missionary;* • *. . . you will bring the light of the gospel to many.*
• *honor your priesthood, study the scriptures, and develop the skills God has given you . . .* • *be active in civic affairs* • *be prompt and dependable* • *come to know Jesus Christ* • *remain worthy, keep yourself apart from the lusts of the world, put your family first . . .* • *always seek the best*	• *. . . and you will receive many opportunities to lead, both inside and outside the Church.* • *. . . and you will find a choice companion and be sealed in the temple and raise a choice family.*

Craig also tried to list his gifts*:*
1. *music*
2. *making friends and talking to people*
3. *feeling the spirit*
4. *sense of humor, love of life*

The options*, at that point, for Craig were pretty simple:*
1. *Go to university for a year, then on a mission.*
2. *Don't go to university, do go on a mission.*
3. *Go to college, don't go on a mission.*
4. *Don't go to college, don't go on a mission.*

As Craig sought advice, he noticed two things: First, the people he admired most all seemed to agree that his education was extremely important and that the kind of service a mission allows is a noble and worthy thing. Second, positive advice about going on a mission and going to school always made him feel two emotions—excitement and a little bit of

*fear. Negative advice on either made him feel easy, but
unchallenged and unexcited.*

*With the things he had listed, Craig pretty much knew what his
direction had to be. Prayer confirmed that direction for him
and gave him a tiny flame of deep inner confidence that he
could do (and do well) what he had decided to do.*

*Note: As Craig's life unfolded, he continually updated and
expanded his "Step 1." Progressively his understanding of
his patriarchal blessing grew and his recognition of (and
possession of) personal gifts increased. Proportionately
his options expanded.*

Step 2–Decision Making

There are essentially two types of decisions in life,
and the second step in *life planning* is to make
each of them correctly. The first type is the
"right-wrong" decision, the kind that has
only two alternatives, one of which you know to be
right, the other wrong. These should be the
easy decisions of life, but they are often the ones that
destroy. The other type of decision is the
multi-alternative decision where we don't yet even
know all the alternatives. The first type of
decisions should be made in *advance*, long before it
is actually faced. The second type should be
made on the basis of the ninth section of the
Doctrine and Covenants, which suggests that
one study out and analyze the possibilities; come to
the best, most prayerful, and most careful
decision he is capable of; and take his decision to the
Lord to seek confirmation or reassurance that
the decision is correct.

The first type includes decisions like getting
married in the temple, paying tithing, filling
Church callings, etc. The second type includes who
to marry, where to live, what occupation to
pursue, etc.

Let's revisit Craig, about three years later, for an
example of Step 2.

Craig's Story, Step 2

*As Craig finishes his mission and is released, his president
mentions to him the small but still alarming percentage of
returned missionaries who don't marry in the temple, who don't
finish their education and who, in one way or another,
partially or totally lose their activity in the Church.*

*Craig decides, during a visit to the temple the day after his
mission release, to make certain decisions in advance—and to
write them out in specific detail in the privacy of his
journal. He spends a full day at it, in an attitude of fasting and
prayer, and the completed (or should we say started) list looks
like this:*

*Craig . . . August 27
Decisions I am prepared to make and commit myself to now:*

1. *Moral cleanliness (no petting or sexual intimacy of
   any kind prior to marriage)*
2. *Temple marriage*
3. *Constant worthy possession of a temple recommend*
4. *Full tithe-paying*
5. *Word of Wisdom observance*
6. *Acceptance of all Church callings*
7. *A private evaluation session every Sunday of my life to
   determine where I am going*
8. *Private prayer every night and morning*
9. *Finish my education*
10. *Attend church every Sunday (priesthood meeting, Sunday
    School, and sacrament meeting)*
11. *Make no major decision without confirmation from the
    Lord*

*Signed,
Craig Archibald*

*Craig takes the list very seriously. He attempts to think through
the most adverse conditions possible and commits
himself to hold to the decision even in those conditions. (For
example, he imagines a time when he is married and still in
school—with a new baby, with bills—and has the temptation and
inclination to defer payment of tithing until the
following year, when he will be graduated and will have a
steady job. He commits himself to make the decision to pay
tithing even in that condition.) Craig signs the list and puts a
date on it; and as he does he feels a remarkable
reassurance that what he has done is right and that he has
literally saved himself the effort of having to make those same
decisions over and over throughout the rest of his life. He knows
the list is not complete yet, that he will have to add to it as
he learns more of life, but he also knows, deep down, that it is a
start—a good start.*

*As Craig's life develops, he quickly begins to come to the second
type of decisions. For example, he's not sure what he
should major in. His views and ideas as well as his
self-confidence have changed since he was last in school; he
is no longer certain he knows what he should do. He goes back to
Step 1 and reevaluates the advice of his patriarchal
blessing and redrafts his list of gifts. He seeks advice from
several people he admires; he literally reads the entire
catalog of courses offered by the university. After the first
semester, he feels he has refined his list of possible majors
down to four or five. He spends the next semester exploring these
and seeking further advice. In the process he exposes his
mind to some interesting things and gradually comes to feel that
his decision is clear. After fasting and prayer he takes
that decision to the Lord and feels the warm, simple assurance
that it is all right.*

60

*Craig follows the same kind of pattern on other
"multi-alternative" decisions. The most important, in
his mind, is marriage, and he partakes of the eternally valuable
experience (along with Connie, the girl he has fallen in love
with) of feeling the Lord's confirmation of their decision to
spend eternity together.*

Two notes relate to this part of Craig's story:

*1. During his courtship with Connie, Craig had a
particularly vivid experience that he will never forget. He was
alone in a car with her in an atmosphere of intense
emotion and physical attraction. At an earlier time, when Craig
was listing in his journal the decisions he was prepared to
make in advance, he had tried to imagine just this setting and
had specifically decided what to say and what to do to
ensure that things did not go too far. Somehow, that came back
to him now, and he reached out his hand to the key, started
the car, and drove Connie home. He realized as he drove home
himself that if he had not made the right decision in
advance, he would have made the wrong one at the moment.*

*2. Five years after their marriage, Craig and Connie had a
major marital crisis. It was a disagreement over how to handle a
matter in Connie's family, and it got progressively worse
until they literally could not communicate any longer. Finally,
at the point where threats of separation were about to be
made and irretrievably harmful things were about to be said, they
both thought back on the time when the Lord had
confirmed the rightness of their marriage to each other. Neither
could deny that that feeling had been profound and real. Its
remembrance took the fight out of the crisis category; it made
them realize they could work it out; and it got them on
their knees to seek the Lord's help. After it was over, they both
realized that without that confirmation they could have*

Step 3–Five-Year Goals

Setting true goals is a remarkable process whereby one begins a thing not at the beginning but at the end. He begins *with* the end; he started out by knowing where he wants to end up.

When a goal is deeply implanted in our minds we become almost like a guided missile, a heat-seeking rocket, or a sound-sensing torpedo that corrects its course and hones in on its target until it reaches it. The appropriate saying goes, "Beware of what you truly want, for you will get it."

61

In the days before we had modern harbors, ships had to anchor outside a port until a flood tide came to carry them in. The ships thus at anchor were described in Latin as being *ab portu*, or in front of the port. As the time for the turning of the tide approached, the captain and crew would take their places. All were alerted as the tide reached its crest, and at the exact moment *all* sprang into action.

They knew that if they missed this tide, they would have to wait for another one; they would thus lose the advantage of being first with their cargo in the market. When we set goals and really want them, we are able to ride the tide when it comes; we are prepared to make things happen. Shakespeare caught this idea in one of his great works.

There is a tide in the affairs of men,
Which, taken at the flood, leads on to fortune;
Omitted, all the voyage of their life
Is bound in shallows and in miseries.
                              (*Julius Caesar*, IV, iii, 217.)

We create our own "breaks." "We become what we think about." "As a man thinketh in his heart, so is he." (See Proverbs 23:7.) Goals are real, and one who knows how to use them can achieve infinitely more than one who does not. William Wrigley, Jr., was a young soap salesman who gave a piece of gum to every purchaser of his soap. He soon noticed that his customers were more eager to get the gum than the soap. He recognized an opportunity. He seized it. He became a manufacturer of chewing gum and a millionaire many times over.

62

Step 3 is the careful, prayerful, persistent setting of five-year goals. One might ask, "Why *five* years? Why not forty or twenty or ten to start out with?" The answer comes in three parts: First, most of us can't think realistically beyond five years (even that seems like quite a stretch). Second, the "directions" we've set (step 1) are a form of longer-range goals that prepare us for looking at the following five years. Third (and most importantly), the Lord usually does not let us in on the future—especially not on our own specific future—enough to give us much to go on beyond a few years. We may pray to understand our foreordination and his wishes for our lives, but his way is usually to prompt us to make the right decision only on the *next* step and then to trust that he will give us more guidance *later*, when we face the following step. This is the essence of the principle we call faith, a principle that is beautifully described in the well-known but anonymous verse:

I said to the man who stood at the gate of years, "Give me a light that I may step forth," and the voice came back to me, "Step out into the darkness and put your hand in mine . . . for that is better than a light and surer than a known way."

It is a little like the engineer of a huge freight train who was asked how he dared speed through

the night with such a limited view of the track ahead.
"Well," he said, "my headlamp lights the
track for two hundred yards, so I just travel that two
hundred yards with the faith that when I get to
the end of it I'll see the next two hundred yards."
This is how our lives go. This is how the Lord
wants them to go because the need for faith is
preserved. For most of us, "two hundred
yards" is about five years. It may not always be
precisely five years. Our lives usually fall into
somewhat natural "eras": three years until
graduation; five years until retirement; six years
before I turn forty, and so on.

The process of setting five-year goals is a lot like
turning a lens slowly and steadily into focus. It
is very difficult at first, even with the help of Step 1
and Step 2, to arrive at meaningful and
specific five-year goals. The images and hopes are
there, but only in blurred outline and diffused
color. With effort, the mind's lens can be turned
gradually into sharp focus.

The process begins with the simple exercise of
trying to imagine where and what you would like to
be on a specific date five years (or
thereabouts) from today: What would you like to
have accomplished? What would you like to be
able to do? What sort of person would you like to
be? What kind of relationships would you
like to have with your friends, with your family,
with yourself, with God? What sort of
environment would you like to be in, at home, at
work? The answers to these questions seem
very much like dreams at first; but that *is* the process
of *life planning*—to turn dreams into goals, goals
into plans, and plans into realities.

Sometimes people ask, and with good reason, "Is it
really necessary to do all this planning? Isn't it
enough just to live the gospel, to be obedient, to do
what the Lord asks?" Such questions are
themselves paradoxes, because the Lord *does* ask us

to set goals, and fully living the gospel implies planning and charting our life's course. One of the Lord's central admonitions literally rings with the implication of thoughtful goals and planned effort: *"Work out your own salvation."* (Philippians 2:12; italics added.) Certainly the meaning of "working out" has a great deal to do with thinking, with analyzing, with *goals* and *plans*. All through the scriptures we are told how God "brings things to pass," and we are admonished to do likewise.

64

There is no question whatever that the Lord wants us to set goals—but there is also no question that we must do it prayerfully and in harmony with *his* will and *our* foreordination. Again, a goal is a powerful thing, a *force* which, if in harmony with God, will work for good and which, if out of step with his will, will damage or at least detour our lives and perhaps the lives of others as well. The scriptures give us this warning: "Go to now, ye that say, To day or to morrow we will go into such a city, and continue there a year. . . . Ye know not what shall be on the morrow . . . for that ye *ought* to say, *if the Lord will*, we shall live, and do this, or that." (James 4:13-15; italics added.)

The message is clear: put the Lord in control of your life; set only those plans that fit *his* pattern; and be prepared, at any time, to abandon your direction if he calls you, through his priesthood, to take another course. Quite often spiritual calls come ahead of planned goals. Some time ago a call was issued to a fine young man to preside over a mission. It wasn't in his timetable, and he responded, "Would it be possible to reissue the call in another three years?" The call didn't come.

Now let's look at Craig again and see how he has put this idea of five-year goals to work:

Craig's Story, Step 3

*Five years have passed. Craig and Connie did get married; Craig
graduated two years later and took a job in an accounting
firm. Their second child (another boy) was born last year and
the minor marital crisis which could have been a major
one (mentioned in the last episode) has just passed. That crisis
was one of the factors that have caused Craig and Connie
to come to grips with their future plans a little more specifically
than they had earlier done. Their views are clearer now
than ever before about where they want to live and the kind of life
they want to lead. Last fast Sunday they made a deep and
genuine effort to spell out where they want to go with the second
five years of their marriage–and where they want to be
when that five years is over. In the process, they both realized
that all the answers won't come in one session, but this list is
the beginning of their goals:*

A. *What we hope to have* done–
   1. *In our family:*
      a. *Have two or three more children (the Lord willing)*
      b. *Own our own home with a mortgage that represents
         less that 1/5 of our income.*
      c. *Rebuild a closer personal relationship with both
         sets of parents in the West (see them each at least twice a
         year)*
      d. *Feel that Craig, Jr., and Richard are well-adjusted and
         happy in school*

   2. *In Craig's career:*
      a. *Finish a graduate degree in management (from
         night school) and move out of accounting and into the
         general management of this or another
         company (have a job with a future)*
      b. *Be comfortable enough financially that we can do
         "c" above without strain*
      c. *Have a net worth of at least $50,000
         (including our house equity and other investments)*

   3. *In Church:*
      a. *Complete our four-generation sheets and have our
         pedigree sheets completed as far back as we can
         go with existing records.*
      b. *Have several families friendshipped, taught by the
         missionaries and brought into the Church*
      c. *Feel satisfied about the filling of any and all
         Church callings received by then*

B. *What we hope to have–*
   1. *In our family:*
      a. *A peace and a harmony and a sense of order
         always prevailing in our home*

b. *Special and individual relationships with* each *of our children*

c. *An ever-growing relationship of love with each other*

2. *In Craig's career:*
   a. *Confidence in writing and speaking*
   b. *An ability to be confident and clear-headed in the presence of my superiors*
   c. *A viable idea for a business of my own sometime in the following five years*
   d. *A deeper knowledge of my own ability*

3. *In the Church:*
   a. *A much stronger working knowledge of the scriptures, a completed chronological outline, compiled together, of each of the standard works*
   b. *A deeper relationship with the Lord and a feeling of intimacy with the Savior*
   c. *Mission calls for the priests in the quorum Craig advises*

Craig and Connie have begun to set aside an hour early in the morning each Sunday, before the children wake up, when they meditate about the direction of their lives, trying to focus the lens. They use their five-year goals as a beacon to help them plan the immediate week ahead.

The principal reason for the five-year goals, of course, is what Craig and Connie are finding out—to provide a *framework* within which to set consistent shorter-term goals and plans.

The trouble with their scheme is that they are "mixing apples and oranges"—they have made a very useful division by separating the goals into three categories: family, Church, and "world" or career, but they also have some very different *kinds* of goals that require different kinds of thinking all lumped together on the same list. The goals of finishing a graduate course or of obtaining a net worth of $50,000 or of finishing a chronological outline of the scriptures are *measurable achievement*-type goals. Not only will Craig and Connie know precisely when they reach them, but they can set directly related, shorter-term "stepping-stone" goals that lead unquestionably to those five-year objectives

(e.g., the five-year goal of $50,000 might lead to a
three-year goal of $20,000 which might lead to
a one-year goal of a certain raise in salary, and so
on). But how would you go about measuring
or breaking down a goal like "a deeper knowledge of
my own career ability" or "an ever-growing
relationship with each other"? These are *relative,
relationship* goals that can be measured only
by feelings and that can only be pursued by
developing the kind of attitudes and practices
and habits that lead to them.

In Step 3, therefore, it is necessary to separate and
distinguish between the five-year *achievement
goals* and the five-year *relationship goals*. There are
probably many good ways to do that. Go with
what feels most comfortable to you. But don't
forget priorities. Too often we work too hard
on achievement, on getting things done, on gaining
material things. Things are the antithesis of
people; and that's the choice we so often face:
People or things, relationships or achievements?
Both have their place, but why is it that we usually
choose the thing over the person—even
when we know that the thing is temporary and the
person is forever? It is important that goals be
put in order of priority.

When Craig and Connie's goals reach a state of
refinement they must further break them down
to the level of *yearly, monthly* and *weekly* objectives.
We'll deal with that in the next section.

But first we'd like to give you a key to making
your goals really effective. That key is simply using
the Sabbath in your goal setting. The
Sabbath is the time to spiritually create our lives, to
get the course of our goals and our plans.

We mentioned earlier that the whole earth
and everything in it and on it serves as an object
lesson. It's the Lord's way of teaching us

spiritual principles that are hard to understand
without temporal analogies. The *origin* of
the earth provides a striking and dramatic example
of the Lord's own pattern for creating and
recreating. God labored and created the world in
six creative periods and then, in the seventh
"day," he rested, re-created, and probably
evaluated and planned the next period. (We
know from the scripture in Moses 3:5 that there was
a Sabbath or planning "day" *before* the
earth's creation as well as after, a time when he
planned all the things that were later put
"naturally" upon the earth.)

68

The scriptures tell us that man was not made for
the Sabbath, but the Sabbath was made for
man. (See Mark 2:27.) And so it was. It is a time to
rest from physical labor and worldly
pursuits, a time to reassess, a time to evaluate the
past, and plan the future, a time to seek
inspiration and explore foreordination.

We hear so much about what *not* to do on
Sunday—different people have given us an
almost Pharisee-like list of "shalt-nots" ranging
from movies to mountain climbing. Would
not the Savior, as he always did, take the more
positive approach, and tell us what *to* do? And
on that list would appear, along with going to
church and studying the scriptures,
meditation, reevaluating, and *planning.* The Sabbath
should be the time to "counsel with the Lord in
all [our] doings" (Alma 37:37), and to seek counsel
and direction from our partner as we
evaluate.

There is a great deal more to the commandment
"*Remember the Sabbath day*" (see Exodus 20:8)
than we are generally aware of. Prophets have
related its observance to the well-being of the
world and have linked Sabbath-breaking with the
occurrence of natural calamities. (See
Spencer W. Kimball, *Ensign*, May 1977, pp. 4-6.) It is

as though the very real and sensitive Life Planning mechanisms of the earth are upset and adversely affected when its inhabitants violate the law of the seventh day.

Most of the Ten Commandments deal with our relationships with other people. The Sabbath day commandment seems to deal directly with our relationship with the earth and with the earth's Creator. One feels, when thinking in this vein and when pondering the tremendous power that can come from proper use of the Sabbath, *that perhaps truly living this commandment is a great key to observance and harmony with all other commandments.*

When we recognize that, each Sunday will become for us, as it is in the Lord's eyes, the day of *re*-creation, the day for turning the lens into focus, a little turn at a time, until our goals take on the focused image of real spiritual creations.

Sunday, then, is a vitally important time for planning and evaluating. Here are some principles or guidelines that can make our Sunday sessions meaningful:

1. It is important to concentrate, to be away from distractions, from telephones, from interruptions. A private place or an early hour (or both) provide the way to achieve this.

2. The quality and beauty of the place you are in will affect the quality and beauty of the thoughts you have. Depending on the season and circumstance, you may want to have your Sunday session in the forest or in the garden or in the most restful room in your house.

3. Begin and end with prayer. The essence of a Sunday session is that it is a time when you put yourself in position and in tune enough to freely

receive the Lord's will for your life and for
the period ahead.

4. Always follow the steps of *life planning* and keep
them in order. First, *Step 1* (at least a brief
glance at your blessing, your list of gifts, etc.). Then
Step 2 (a review of the "type 1" decisions made in
advance and a look at the "type 2" decisions coming
up). Then *Step 3* (a review and refinement of
your five-year goals). Then *Steps 4* and *5*, which are
discussed next.

Step 4–Stepping-stone Achievement Goals 71

If a human being were put in front of (or beneath)
an elephant and asked whether he thought
he was capable of eating the beast, he would almost
certainly respond in the negative. If, on the
other hand, he were told that he would have to eat
only a small part per day, he would likely
conclude that he could do it.

Often when we confront ourselves with ambitious
"high hopes" of five-year goals, our
inclination is to say "impossible"—until we realize
that it is just a matter of breaking the goal down
and getting there one small step at a time.

If a person can construct five one-year goals that
equal or reach the five-year goal; if he can then
lay out twelve one-month goals that total the
one-year goal; if he can then plan four
one-week objectives that get to the monthly goal;
and if he can *reach* the weekly goals each
week—then, presto! He *can* eat an elephant. This is
what Sunday sessions are all about: breaking
goals down so that they will add up. This is the
process of Step 4.

New Year's resolutions have a rather bad
name in some quarters. Their reputation is

tarnished because they are usually forgotten
with as little thought as they were set. *New year goals*,
on the other hand, are an indispensable part
of planning your life. The Christmas holidays, busy
as they are, often provide the ideal time to set
yearly goals. The days between Christmas Day and
New Year's Day usually contain enough
spare time for some prayerful thought and some
fasting (fasting would be well advised after all
the Christmas feasting even if it were *not* necessary
to effectively transpose five-year goals into
one-year goals).

72

Once the one-year goals are set, monthly planning
becomes meaningful. Almost as though the
Lord were designing a perfect time for us to
accomplish this, he has given us *fast Sunday*.
This first Sunday, while fasting, is the ideal time to
prayerfully transpose yearly objectives to
monthly ones. *Again, as on each Sunday, it is wise to first
go through Steps 1, 2, and 3, then to review and refine
the yearly goals, then to create the monthly overview.*

Craig's Story–Step 4

*It is summertime now and Craig and Connie are more involved
than ever with the fast pace of their lives. It's the third of July
today, fast Sunday, and Craig has slipped up into the canyon
for his Sunday session. Connie will have hers after
Church while he watches the children, and they will compare
notes later that evening. After a prayer, Craig takes a half
hour or so to review the things he keeps in his Sunday session
folder. They are essentially the things from Steps 1, 2,
and 3: the blessings, the lists, and the five- and one-year goals.
He is always amazed at how he gets a little closer to reaching
those goals each week; he's also amazed at the fact that they seem
to be refined and clarified and made more specific every
week. He spends the second half hour developing and
simplifying his goals for the upcoming month.*

It is the *weekly* "stepping-stone" that involves the real
planning. By the time we get right up to the week

ahead, we know our schedule, our appointments,
the requirements on our time. These,
together with our monthly goals, allow us to carve
out a plan that will actually move us toward our
objectives. The challenge of weekly planning is to be
disciplined but not rigid, goal-conscious but
not goal-obsessed. The key is to adopt an attitude of
"serendipity." Serendipity is defined as "the
capacity, through good fortune and sagacity
(sensitive observation) of being able to
discover something good while looking for
something else." A shorter definition would be
"a happy accident." The spontaneous moments of
life are the source of much joy. A
well-planned week not only allows for them, it
encourages them, because the mind of a man with
solid objectives and plans is clear of anxiety and
moment-to-moment crisis and can therefore
better observe and better respond to unexpected
opportunities, spontaneous moments, and
"happy accidents."

Weekly planning basically involves the scheduling
of a person's time to meet *objectives* as well as
obligations, and to do the things he *wants* to do as
well as the things he *needs* to do. Weekly
planning is the natural "next step" to take each
Sunday after Steps 1, 2, and 3 have been
reviewed and the yearly and monthly goals looked at
and remembered.

Weekly goals and plans are essential because they
are the key to *getting things done*, and we live in a
time when there is a great deal to do. The age and
the time in which we live require much more
than mere *observation* of life. We are not here as
spectators; we are key *participants* on the stage of
life. We are here to play leading roles in the
concluding act of the drama of the second
estate.

Craig's Story–Step 4 Continued

It is a couple of weeks later. Craig has developed a simple form that helps him to plan his week quickly and effectively. The one he has completed today looks like the accompanying chart.

Week of July 17-23

hold family home evening on not quarreling / buy plane tickets (circle)

invite Barney (nonmember) to Church / do 2 endowments at temple (triangle)

mail application / see John for advice on how to ask for raise (square)

Sunday	Monday	Tuesday	Wednesday	Thursday	Friday	Saturday
Sunday session	Office	Office	Office	Office	Office	kids on "daddy date" to McDonalds while Connie does shopping
Priesthood meeting						
Sunday School		lunch see John	lunch buy	lunch with		
Call Barney		about advice	tickets	Connie		family to Burke Lake (rent boat)
Connie's Sunday session						
Sacrament meeting	FHE (quarreling)	temple	babysit (Connie at Relief Society)	finish grad-school application	"Date" with Connie	

Craig has found it helpful to have a shape symbol for each of the three areas of his achievement goals. The circle signifies the family, the triangle stands for Church, and the square box contains the "world-oriented" weekly goals.

A true story illustrates this point. The story is about a basketball coach we will call Bill. He had not originally been a coach but a high school English teacher in a small school in Wyoming. The school lost their regular coach at the beginning of the season, and Bill was asked to take over. The team got off to a miserable start, losing their first eight games, largely because of the lackadaisical, self-satisfied attitude of the team's two tallest and most-experienced "stars." The two boys were sons of the town's two leading families and felt little need to prove themselves to anyone or to exert full effort.

As the team continued to lose, the townspeople became rather upset. Bill received some nasty notes and a lot of dirty looks. Even though he didn't consider himself to be a coach, his pride was affected and he made up his mind to turn things around. He honestly assessed what was necessary and began to plan the rest of the season, week by week. The next day he told his two stars that they would either have to do it his way or quit. They quit. Bill brought up two green sophomores to fill their places, and the team really went to work. They won their next game—and four out of the next five. The team made up for lack of height and experience with careful planning and sheer determination. They kept winning. To everyone's surprise (including Bill's) when the regular season ended they were in third place in their league and had qualified (just barely) for the regional tournament. By sheer guts and effort (and a lot of homework about the other teams) they finished third in the regional tournament and qualified (just barely) for the state tournament. Then a miracle happened. Every player played above his head every day of the tournament and, when the smoke cleared, there they were, hardly able to believe it, the state champions!

Bill says he remembers so well, as they were carried off the arena floor on the shoulders of the

screaming fans, that he looked way up at the back of
the hall on the back row of the bleachers and
saw, sitting there all alone, the two boys who had quit
the team early in the season when their record
was 0-8.

Theodore Roosevelt teaches the same lesson in his
own exciting way: "In the battle of *life*, it is not
the critic who counts, not the man who points out
where the strong man stumbled or where the
doer of the deed could have done better. The credit
belongs to the man who is actually *in* the arena;
whose face is marred by blood and sweat, who
knows the great efforts, the deep feelings,
who strives valiantly, and falls short again and
again (because there is no effort without
failure), who, in the end, if he succeeds, knows the
triumph of high achievement; and if he fails,
at least fails while *daring greatly*, so that his place will
never be among those cold and timid souls who
never knew either victory or defeat."

Life is a battle; and it *is* the man in the arena who
counts. *Life planning*, particularly the diligent
"Sunday sessions" that plan each week and make
that week effective, is the key not only to
being in the arena, but to winning far more than we
lose.

Daily planning is a simple matter, once we've
made our weekly plans. Daily planning should
happen each evening just before evening
prayer (i.e., plan *tomorrow* each night before
retiring). Such planning accomplishes two
important and specific purposes: (1) It gets right
down to the specifics in terms of time and place
and little details that need remembering (it's better
than a string tied around your finger). (2) It
makes our daily prayers more meaningful, because
instead of the general, tired phrases we often
use over and over in prayers, we start praying about
particular and timely things that are going to
happen *tomorrow*; we start asking for help and
further inspiration on things we have worked

out through careful thought. Thus our prayer is more thoughtful, more effective, and certainly more pleasing to the Lord.

Craig's Story—Step 4 Concluded

It is Monday night. Craig and Connie have had an enjoyable family home evening and are ready for bed. They kneel down and pause for five minutes to think about the coming day before they start their prayer. On the bed in front of them is the weekly planner and a simple blank sheet on which to compare notes for the coming day. After they fill it out it looks like this:

Date: Monday, July 13

	Craig	Connie
7:00	Arise—prayer jog—shower	Arise—prayer Get Craig, Jr., ready for nursery school
8:00	Breakfast	Breakfast
9:00	Drop off Craig, Jr. Office	Take Richard in for immunization shots
10:00	(Finish Bradley account)	Clean house—bedrooms
11:00		Pick up Craig, Jr.
12:00	Lunch with John (advice on asking Fred for a raise)	Lunch with kids
1:00		Take Craig, Jr., in for new shoes
2:00		
3:00	Start Thompson tax calculations	Prepare dinner
4:00		
5:00		
6:00	Dinner	Dinner
7:00	Leave for temple	Get babysitter— leave for temple
8:00		
9:00		
10:00	Drive babysitter home	
11:00	Read scriptures together—plan Tuesday—prayer	

It is through the implementation of *daily* plans that we actually begin to "eat the elephant." The weekly goals are a framework and a guide (just as the monthly goals were for them), but it is the daily plans that we actually implement.

There really is no tomorrow—tomorrow never comes—only an endless succession of todays. It is *this* day that counts, this day that we can really *do* something about. The Sanskrit poet had a particularly beautiful way of saying it:

Yesterday is but a dream and tomorrow but a vision, but today, well lived, makes every yesterday a dream of joy and every tomorrow a vision of hope.

An eminently successful football coach, perhaps the "winningest" coach in the National Football League's history, used to have a motto which, in its own way, says basically the same thing: "The future is *now*."

President N. Eldon Tanner tells how, as a teenager, he developed the practice of beginning his evening prayers by reporting to the Lord what he had accomplished during the day he'd just completed. Then, after making that report, he felt more justified in asking for help on the things he hoped to do the following day. I believe it is a pattern he has followed ever since. It is also precisely the pattern suggested by the daily planning part of *life planning*.

Often the problem that arises most obviously in daily planning is simply that we have more things that need doing than can possibly *be* done in one day. The key, of course, is *prioritizing*. When you plan the day and list the objectives, list them in order of their importance and pursue them in that order.

When you prioritize, it is essential to differentiate between *importance* and *urgency*.

Some things are important but not urgent
(i.e., helping your daughter get more excited about
starting school next fall). Other things are
urgent but not really very important (i.e., fixing the
door that keeps banging or preparing a
special appetizer for the important guests that are
coming tonight). This, then, is how you should
order your priorities when you plan your day:
1. Things that are important *and* urgent.
2. Things that are urgent but not important.
3. Things that are important but not urgent.
4. Things that are neither important nor urgent.

Let us reiterate: Through daily planning followed
by kneeling prayer, one can make
communication with the Lord more specific and
thus more effective.

Richard Eyre had an experience many years
ago that vividly impressed his mind with the
importance of *two-way communication* in
prayer. I was a missionary at the time, he recalls, and
one evening as we were about to retire, my
companion and I heard a knock at our door. We
opened it and were surprised to see a
General Authority of the Church, a great man
whom we both respected deeply. (He had
spoken to the missionaries earlier in the week and
was staying just down the hall in the same
building we lived in.) He said, simply, "May I join
you for evening prayer?" We invited him in and
knelt together by the couch. He invited me to offer
the prayer. In the middle of the prayer I
began to hear the unmistakable scratch of a pencil
writing rapidly on paper. My first thought was,
"What on earth is my companion doing?" I went on
with the prayer, and the scratching noises
continued from time to time. When I closed, and
looked up, I was amazed to find that it was not
my companion but the General Authority who had
been writing. I didn't say anything but I
guess he noted the look on my face and as he got up
to leave he answered my nonverbal question

with a question of his own, "If you had the privilege
of speaking with the prophet and asking him
some important questions, don't you think you
would take notes? We've just been talking to the
Lord. I usually take notes right after the prayer but
my memory isn't always that good."

I remember lying awake most of that night
thinking that I had just learned what prayer really is.

The daily planning part of life planning is a way of
talking directly and specifically with the Lord
about things of immediate interest. And it is a joy to
alter or add to your plan after speaking with
and "hearing from" the Lord.

The Fill-in-the-Dot System for "Achievement Goals"

The old adage that success breeds success is very
true. Succeeding and getting things done can
become a habit just as surely as can failing or
procrastinating. As we pursue daily and
weekly achievement goals, it is important that we
have a "check-off" system of some sort, a
method of indicating (and congratulating ourselves)
when an objective is achieved.

One of the simplest and best methods for doing
this is the fill-in-the-dot system. This involves
simply putting a circle next to each written
objective on the daily and weekly planning sheets.
When that item is accomplished the circle is
shaded in and changes from this ○ to this ●. Once
the circle has been filled in, the plan has
become reality; the thought has become substance;
the void has been filled.

You will be amazed at the satisfaction and
pleasure that can come from the simple act of
filling in a circle.

The circles are also valuable on the monthly
and yearly goal lists—and even on the five-year list.

On these the circles need to be a little bigger so
that they can be *progressively* shaded in as time
passes and as accomplished weekly goals
bring one closer and closer to the longer-term
objectives. After three months or so, a yearly
circle might look like this ◖. If it was mostly
accomplished in the next few months, it
would have gradually altered to this ◕.

This system is so basic and so easily grasped that it
is also very usable for small children. Four-
and five-year-olds are very capable of
understanding the concept of a simple
objective; and they *truly* comprehend the idea of
achieving it when they use the dot system. We
know a four-year-old who set a goal to learn to tie his
own shoes. His parents helped him to write the
goal on paper and to put a big circle by it. They
thought he had a three- or four-week goal.
But he was so excited about wanting to fill in that
circle that he practiced all day and filled in his
circle that night.

Well, that's all of Step 4. What a lot pf planning:
yearly, monthly, weekly, daily! Isn't it a little too
much? Shouldn't we be worried about the
possibility of "analysis paralysis"?

Well, let's think about it for a minute. There are
168 hours in a week. We're suggesting that you use *2*
of those hours for *life planning* (1 hour for
the weekly planning, the other for daily
planning—7 days at 10 minutes or so per day).
Two hours, then, to plan the other 166. Is it worth
it? Maybe the best answer comes in the form
of an analogy: Have you ever tried to saw a board
with a very dull saw? The saw goes back and
forth; your arm gets tired; there's a lot of noise (and
maybe even a little smoke); but very little
happens to the board. If you extract that saw from
the board and spend a few minutes with a file,
sharpening it, a miraculous thing happens: the saw
develops a *cutting* edge. You put the saw to

wood again and suddenly, smoothly, and with less physical effort, the sawdust pile begins to grow and the board gets cut in two. So it is with planning. The 2 hours you spend "sharpening your saw" will make the other 166 far more effective, far more fun, far more worth living.

Relationship Planning

As illustrated over and over in the preceding pages, 83
our achievements are affected by our relationships.
A balance between success in our relationships
and success in our achievements is crucial. Indeed,
we can say even more than that.
Relationships and achievements are *reliant* on each
other. A man cannot achieve his full potential
without the bracing support and fulfillment of
satisfying relationships—nor can he
participate deeply in real and beneficial
relationships if his achievement needs and
desires are unmet.

It is relationships that we take with us beyond the
grave. (Most achievements are temporary, and
we eventually retain only the learning that they may
have provided.) Relationship goals,
however, do not lend themselves to the kind of
"elephant-eating" short-range-leading-
to-long-range type of pursuit that accomplishes
achievement goals. Since they are relative
and measurable only by feelings, goals like "know
the Savior better" or "draw closer as a husband
and wife" cannot be sought by subdivision into
measurable "chunks." Instead they must be
pursued by the alteration of *attitude* and *habit*. This is
essentially done by conscious effort and through
prayer—and through "programming" the
subconscious mind.

The key principle involved in this "programming" has been stated in a thousand different ways: "the as-if principle"; "as a man thinketh, so is he"; "you are what you think you are." The objective of this section is to give the reader a direct way to apply this principle in becoming the kind of person he wants to be and in developing the kind of relationships he wants to have. The starting point is still Steps 1, 2, and 3, which together yield some general ideas of what you want your relationships to become.

Step 5–Programming the Mind to Develop Stronger Relationships

Step 5 basically involves taking our general relationship goals and making them specific, then developing practices and habits that bring about and continually improve the relationships we desire. The process is as follows:

First: Write "future relationship" descriptions. Sit down and try to *describe* the relationship you feel you would like to have in a year's time with one of your children, or with your wife, or with yourself. As an example, let's look at Craig's effort to do this in terms of the relationship he wants to have with one of his sons.

Craig's Story–Step 5

Time has been passing at Craig and Connie's home. The older two children are now in school and there are two more in the family, a four-year-old boy named Mac and (at last) a new little daughter. Craig is aware that Mac isn't a little baby anymore, and he feels the importance of establishing a unique relationship with him. In an effort to pinpoint the kind of relationship he hopes to develop, Craig writes the following description of an imaginary event exactly a year from now:

Sitting on a sandbar at the edge of the river. Mac holding his fishing pole, waiting a record-long three minutes for another jerk. (He caught his first "all by myself" fish five minutes ago: "Get him off the hook, Dad, so I can catch another one!")

"Mac, you are my favorite fishing buddy."

"What about your brother, Dad?"

*"Well, Mac, he's just my brother. You are my son and
my brother. Do you know what that means?"*

*"Yes, Dad. Hey, I saw another fish down there . . . come
on . . . come and bite!" (Ten minutes pass . . . no bites.)*
"Dad, I think I can throw a rock all the way across."

"OK, son, but if you miss you'll scare the fish."

"I can, Dad!"

"OK, try it, son."

"See, it was easy—I'm going to try a bigger one."

*There is an openness, a freeness, an easy-ness when we are
together. He feels no pressure to prove that he's good, because
he senses that I couldn't love him any more no matter what he
did. Already we have begun to feel like a team. We're
unbeatable together! His pride in me matches mine for him.*

85

"Mac, tell me how you're doing in kindergarten lately."

"Great, Dad. I love it."

"How are you doing on the lessons?"

"Fine. They're easy."

*"Mac, that's why you've got to do your best—because it's easy.
Do you understand?"*

"Yes, Dad. Why don't these fish bite any more?"

*"I guess you caught the only one in this river, Mac. Race me to
the car?"*

"OK, Dad. I'll beat ya!"

Simple descriptions of what we hope our
relationships will become are of great value in
helping our minds understand the kind of efforts
we need to make and the kind of
communication we need to have. (They can also
develop one's ability to think and write clearly.)
These written descriptions are then read and
pondered for a few moments each Sunday in
the Sunday session. The pondering will spark
thoughts and ideas as to what can be done *that
week* to strengthen each relationship.

Second: Develop habits. Decide on a basic set of *habits*
(things that you commit yourself to do on a

regular basis) that will build and strengthen your relationships. The simplest example is probably the family home evening habit, which builds family relationships, or the weekly "continue-the-courtship" date with your spouse, which strengthens the communication and bond between husband and wife. Be careful not to overdo it. There is only a certain amount of available time in the week and too many "programs" or ideas will be discouraging and frustrating rather than becoming the simple, reliable, predictable "relationship times" that one looks forward to with real anticipation. The idea is workable for any age or situation but Craig's example is a pretty good and pretty general one:

Craig's Story–Step 5 Continued

As their family developed, Craig and Connie felt a growing need to hold fast to certain habits that they knew were good for their relationships . . . and to build other traditions or practices to strengthen areas they did not feel satisfied with. They finally came up with twelve "flip cards" that they looked at and used to check themselves each week during their Sunday session. The cards were categorized under family, God *and* self.

A. Family Relationships

1. *Make Home a Heaven* *Oneness* in marriage *Stewardship* with children	2. *Oneness in Marriage* • "date" each Friday night • "good turn" for each other daily • "Sunday session" together each week

3. *Stewardship with Children* • Family home evening each Monday • "Daddy date" or "Mommy date" with each child every two weeks	4. *Reinforce:* Family laws Family traditions Family pride Family order Family unity

1. *Returning to Him* Knowing, loving, and being like Christ asking and listening studying and understanding	2. *Studying and Understanding* • read scriptures fifteen minutes each day
3. *Asking and Listening* • family prayer each evening at dinner • prayer as husband and wife each night • private prayer each morning	4. *Knowing and Loving Christ* • *prepare* for the sacrament each Sunday morning

C. Relationship with Self

1. *"Foreordination"* How are you? Where are you? What are you becoming?	2. *How Are You?* • physically (jog four times a week) • mentally (read a book a month) • emotionally (time with hobbies)
3. *Where Are You?* • read patriarchal blessing each fast Sunday • write in journal at least weekly	4. *What Are You Becoming?* • Sunday session every Sunday • plan before prayer every night

Craig and Connie found that it took only a few minutes each Sunday to flip through the twelve cards together. They did so with a note pad in hand, making notes on any "habits" that they have let down on or that need particular attention during the coming week.

At the moment, Craig is thinking about putting the twelve cards on 35mm slides so they can be projected on the wall each Sunday session and thus "gone through" more quickly and effectively.

Third: Mentally review the qualities you want. Develop a list of the *qualities you wish* to obtain—a simple word-by-word description of the kind of person

you want to be and the specific qualities you
want to exhibit in your relationships with others,
with your family, and with God.

Benjamin Franklin had a method that
helped him do this. He created a list of the personal
attributes he wanted to gain and worked on
them until they were a part of him. We are
suggesting that you expand that idea: list the
attributes you want to develop; but also describe
the kind of person you want to be (and thus the
qualities you want to give) to your wife, to your
children, and to the Lord—as well as to
yourself.

88

This concept is made simple by example:

Craig's Story—Step 5 Concluded
*As his life continued to take shape, Craig found himself becoming
more and more aware of the gaps between the sort of person
he was and the sort of person he wanted to be. He applied Step 5
of life planning as follows:*
Keys in My Relationship with Connie (the 5 Ps)
1. Priority (*Think of her* first *in all I do.*)
2. Partner (*Include her in my thoughts, our dreams.*)
3. 'Preciate (*Compliment her,* notice *her great
   qualities.*)
4. Pamper (*Make her feel delicate, needed, loved, special.*)
5. Plan, Pray (*Plan together each night, know* her *goals each
   day.*)

Keys to My Relationship with the Children (The 5 Cs)
1. Confidence (*Make them always aware of my faith
   and trust in them.*)
2. "Consultant" (*Don't always control and manage
   what they do; observe, and listen, and suggest where
   appropriate.*)
3. Consistent (*Enforce the family laws; be dependable.*)
4. Calm (*Always bring a peaceful spirit into the
   house.*)
5. Collective (*Don't think of them collectively; have an
   individual relationship with each one.*)

Keys in My Relationship with God
1. Faith (*Develop it as a power.*)
2. Hope (*Realize that all depends on Christ.*)
3. Charity (*Try to always ask "What would Christ do?"*)

4. "Thrice—always" (*Pray morning, noon, and night; have a prayer in my heart always.*)

Keys in My Relationships with Others
1. Listen (*And talk about his interests, his expertise.*)
2. Compliment (*Find something to like in everyone–and tell him what it is.*)
3. Remember names (*A person's name is the most important word to him.*)
4. Smile (*It can make someone's day.*)

Key Qualities I Want in My Relationship with Myself
1. "Serendipity" (*To be the kind of person who is observant and sensitive enough to find "happy accidents."*)
2. "Stewardship" (*To be the kind of person who takes proper care of all responsibilities and opportunities.*)
3. "Peaceable" (*To be the kind of person who is calm and collected regardless of circumstance.*)
4. "Pizzazz" (*To be the kind of person who does things well and with individuality–who makes common things uncommon.*)
5. "Light" (*To be the kind of person who seeks truth and is in tune enough to recognize truth's "light" when it is found.*)
6. "Confident humility" (*To be the kind of person who knows he is nothing without the Lord–and everything with Him.*)

Now, the remaining question is, how does one get these "relationship qualities" he has developed off the written list and *into* his actual personality and character so that they really *do* start affecting and improving his relationships and making him a better person?

Well, one way (as with the other parts of Step 5) is to read and think through them during every Sunday session. This is usually not enough, however. There needs to be a direct way to pound them right into the subconcious mind so that they begin to manifest themselves automatically, without conscious effort, in the relationships of our lives.

The following suggested way may at first sound a little strange or unorthodox. Indeed, it *is* unorthodox; but it works—and it actually allows a

person, in only about an hour each week, to
develop himself physically, mentally, emotionally,
socially, and spiritually all at the same time.
The process is as follows:

Go jogging (or exercise) three times a week, for
twenty minutes or so at a time. During the
twenty minutes, while you are running, think
through *each list of words* in your mind, using
them to *describe* the kind of person you are (i.e., "I
am a person who thinks of my wife as a *partner*.
I place my wife in highest *priority*. I *'preciate* my wife,
etc.") As you *describe yourself* with each word,
think quickly of things you have done or are
planning to do that *show* that the word describes
you well. As you tell yourself these things, you will
become these things.

Now you are sure to ask, "Why do it while I am
running?" There is a whole list of interesting
answers:

1. Exercise is good for you. (The jogging and
exercise fad is probably the best fad that has ever
hit America.)

2. Your mind works quicker and more clearly
while you are exercising. (You can think through
the words in less time and with more
alertness.)

3. Something about exercise opens up the
subconscious mind and makes it more
susceptible to the kind of "programming" we are
advocating here. Psychiatrists are discovering
this phenomenon even though they don't pretend
to fully understand it. Some find that their
therapy works better when a patient is jogging than
when he is lying on a couch. Thaddeus
Kostrubala, the author of *The Joy of Running* says,
"I think this [running] is a new and powerful
way of reaching the unconscious."

Time magazine says, "Some psychiatrists now routinely prescribe jogging instead of pills for moderate depression." (July 24, 1978, p. 50.) Dr. Robert S. Brown of the University of Virginia is one of several who think that jogging cures mental problems by changing the chemical composition of the body.

The point is that "thinking" your list of desired relationship qualities *into* your subconscious while exercising *works*.

The summary message of Step 5 is beautiful: One can *decide* what kind of person he wants to be and what kind of relationships he wants to have. Then, by following the simple and not very time-consuming process outlined in *life planning*, he can *be* and *have* what he wants!

The Five Steps of Life Planning in Review

92   ## Step 1 *"direction setting"*

Analyze your situation and point yourself in the direction of your "foreordination."

Tools:
A. Patriarchal blessing
B. List of "gifts"
C. List of "options"
D. Advice
E. Prayer

Step 2 *"decisions"*

Make, in advance, the "right-wrong" decisions of life. List them and sign the list. Follow the process of Doctrine and Covenants section 9 for the "multi-alternative" decisions you cannot make in advance.

Step 3 *"long-range goals"*

Establish five-year goals. Separate the "relationship goals" from the "achievement goals."

Step 4 *"achievement goals"*

Break out one-year goals from the five-year framework. Then create monthly goals that will lead to the yearly, and weekly goals that will lead to the monthly.

Step 5 *"relationship goals"*

*Develop the habits and attitudes that will carry you to
your relationship goals through "advance descriptions" of
what you want your relationships and habits to be.
Think the necessary qualities into your mind during
Sunday sessions and during periods of exercising.*

Sequence of Sunday Sessions:

1. Review and update all tools of Step 1.

2. Review and update the "advance
decisions" list of Step 2.

3. Review and update the long-range relationship
and achievement goals of Step 3.

4. Set specific weekly goals (set monthly goals
on fast Sunday) as Step 4.

5. Recommit and program yourself on the habits
and qualities set up as Step 5.

REVIEW OF PRINCIPLES

Plan to succeed:
what, why, where,
when, who, how?

What?

*Review of
Principles*

Life planning!   97

A simple, workable process for finding and
fulfilling the foreordination that
accompanies each of us to this earth.

A way of *creating* and of "bringing things to pass."

A way of finding more time to do more things.

A way of showing more respect for "mother earth"
and "father time!"

A way of pleasing God, who has instructed us to
"*work out* our own salvation." (See Philippians 2:12.)

A way to draw down his help into our lives.

98   *Because* of that solemn charge to work out our salvation.

Because we were put here to act, not to react, to subdue the earth and *master* ourselves, to *find* and *become* all that is in us.

Because:
*"For of all sad words of tongue or pen,
The saddest are these: 'It might have been!' "*
               (John Greenleaf Whittier)

Because:
*"Life is real! life is earnest!
And the grave is not its goal;
Dust thou art, to dust returnest,
Was not spoken of the soul."*
             (Henry Wadsworth Longfellow)

And because:
*"Lives of great men all remind us
We can make our lives sublime,
And, departing, leave behind us
Footprints on the sands of time."*
                       (Longfellow)

Because too many of us are "always getting ready to live, but never living." (Ralph Waldo Emerson)

Because we cannot "kill time without injuring eternity." (Henry David Thoreau)

Because: "He that lives upon hope will die fasting." *Review of Principles*
(Benjamin Franklin)

And (perhaps most of all) because *life planning* is
a formula for *joy*, in great abundance, both
immediate and eternal.

Where?

100   Here! On this incredibly well-equipped earth where we can handle *things* and measure *time*, where we learn law by natural consequence, and love by bridling our natural affection.

Here! In this place where, according to one apostle, we can learn to conform to the laws of God in a tenth of the time that it takes us to learn them elsewhere (after death). (That apostle, Elder Melvin J. Ballard, went on to explain, "It is much easier to overcome [problems] . . . when both flesh and spirit are combined as one." See "Three Degrees of Glory.")

Here! Where the veil teaches us faith, and faith teaches us to know ourselves.

Here! Where *life planning* can help us to be sure that the self we get to know is the best self we have.

When?

On the Sabbath day, which God made for man that
man might recreate himself, through worship,
through rest, and through *life planning*.

Through the type of "Sunday session" that
sets our destination, then charts our course, then
corrects that course regularly—weekly!

Through this one commandment, one of
ten, the full observance of which straightens the
course to observance of all the others.

On the Sabbath day, *every* Sabbath
day—*now*, as eternity's second hand sweeps toward
the conclusion of earth's eleventh hour.

Who?

---

102   Those who know!

You and all of us who know that the goal of life is
to *return*; and who know that the elements of the
gospel are a potential roadmap if we can just
put it all together right—and read it.

Those who want to be more than they are.

Those who want to grasp the treadmill turmoil of
the world and *order* it into simplified purpose.

Those who want to act rather than react.

Those who truly value this scant spot of time
given us to build the Lord's kingdom by beginning
to build our own.

How?

By the five steps of *life planning*, each step surrounded by prayer and fastened by faith.

Book designed by Michael Clane Graves
Composed by University Services, Inc.
in Baskerville and Baskerville Italic
with display lines in Stencil Bold
Printed by Publishers Press
on 60 # Simpson Antique
Bound by Mountain States Bindery
in Sturdetan "20048" Navy Blue